NUGGETS 2

A GUIDE FOR THOSE

ENGAGED IN MINISTRY

Apostle Joyce Myrick Brown , DCE

E-Book ISBN: 978-1-969066-33-7

Paperback ISBN: 978-1-969066-34-4

Published by

Columbus Book Publishers
www.columbusbookpublishers.com

Printed in the United States of America

Dedication

I dedicate this book to everyone who feels they have experienced a call by God into the work of the ministry. You have come into great company and are surrounded by so great a cloud of witnesses, for all who have embarked onto this journey before you, as well as the thousands upon thousands who now join. You are not unique in the sense that you are alone.

You are encouraged to prove yourself faithful before God in the presence of man, and as stated by Paul in 1 Timothy 6:12,

"Fight the good fight of faith-lay hold on eternal life to which you were also called and have professed the good profession in the presence of many witnesses."

May God bless each of you, and may you ever be found faithful in the work to which God has called, commissioned, and confirmed you to do.

Acknowledgment

I take this time to acknowledge and to thank the following persons for their support and encouragement toward this book, NUGGETS 2 For Women Engaged in Ministry.

I thank Minister Willie Mae Montgomery-Artis for editing the book.

I thank Pastor Charlotte Cody for her prayers for the WEIM, which is included in the Book as The Prayer of Dedication.

I also thank those who have held me uplifted before God in prayer through my various endeavors to accomplish a work so precious that our Father chose to place in my hands.

God Bless you all. I love you.

About the Author

Joyce Myrick Wooden-Brown is a distinguished author known for her compelling storytelling and profound insights into the human experience. With a background that spans various genres, Joyce has captivated readers with her unique voice and ability to weave intricate narratives that resonate on a deep emotional level.

Her journey as a writer began at a young age, fueled by a passion for literature and a keen observation of the world around her. Over the years, Joyce has honed her craft, developing a style that is both engaging and thought-provoking. Her works often explore themes of identity, resilience, and the complexities of relationships, drawing readers into richly imagined worlds that reflect the nuances of real life.

Joyce's dedication to her craft has earned her numerous accolades and a loyal readership. Her books have been praised for their lyrical prose, well-drawn characters, and the ability to evoke a wide range of emotions.

She is a trailblazer in kingdom leadership whose ministry reverberates through the lives she touches. As Senior Pastor of *In God We Trust Ministries Phase II Church* and the visionary Founder & Chancellor of *Kingdom Life Ministries Bible Institute*, she leads with a mantle of truth, grace, and divine assignment.

Her spiritual journey is marked by an enthusiastic commitment to teaching, writing, and developing leaders. Through dynamic sermons, transformative Holy Convocations, and empowering theological education, Joyce cultivates faith and inspires purpose. She is the author of *The Mantle of Ministry: Embracing the Call* and the devotional *Nuggets*, offering scriptural insight wrapped in lyrical prose and lived wisdom.

She also expands her ministry's reach through her radio broadcast *A Time In His Presence*, and contributes to the collaborative devotional *Echoes of Faith*. Her leadership has mentored many into diverse ministry roles—Preacher, Teacher, Facilitator, Worship Leader—equipping them to stand anchored in truth and activated for purpose.

In *Nuggets 2*, Joyce continues her mission: to uplift, enlighten, and equip through inspired reflection, authentic storytelling, and a voice that echoes heaven's call..

Let Us Open with Prayer

Heavenly Father,

We come before You in humble reverence, asking for Your presence to saturate every page of this book. May Nuggets be more than words; it may be nourishment for the soul, encouragement for the weary, and light for the path ahead. Bless the reader with revelation, with clarity, and with an ignited passion to know You deeper. Let each message be a seed planted in fertile hearts, growing into divine understanding and unwavering faith. We invite Your Spirit to speak beyond the ink, to minister beyond our limits, and to transform lives in ways only You can.

Amen.

Table of Contents

Preface i

Introduction iv

Section I: Part A 1

The Challenge of the Call 2

Recognizing the Call 5

The Challenge of Overcoming the Desire of Glamorous or Prestigious Positioning 14

Taking The Step 25

The role of the Evangelist is not limited to a specific gender. Both men and women can be called to this office and serve effectively in this capacity. 28

Section I - Part B Description of Levels of Offices 30

Female-Defined Ministry Workers In the Church of Today 31

Section II Descriptions, Course Requirements and Duties of the Licensed Minister, Ordained Elder, Deacon and the Deaconess 36

Ministry Positions (non-biased gender roles) Acknowledged in the Church of Today 37

The Missionary Pledge 42

The Position of the Deacon & the Deaconess 43

Recommended Course Requirements for Those Engaging in Ministry 47

Section III Required Study Part A 50

Ministry Positions (non-biases gender roles) Acknowledged in the Church of Today 51

Here's Your Interview 54

Worksheets Part B 56

Making Preparation for Ministry 57

Defining Your Spiritual Gifts Worksheet 60

The Statement of Faith Worksheet 63

The Doctrine Why We Believe? What We Believe? 64

Ordinances of the Church 65

The Spiritual Life 67

Spiritual Gifts 70

Protocol Is! "Honor to whom honor is due." (Romans 13:7) 76

Stewardship 78

History of Women in Ministry Then and Now......................................80

Nuggets Of Gold 82

Preface

Knowing Your Purpose

You Were Born for This. God saw and chose you for a special purpose. You were in His mind even before your conception from the very beginning through childhood. Your role and objectives are clear and significant. You have been selected to fulfill important responsibilities. To demonstrate your unique strengths and qualifications. Everything in your life so far has prepared you for this purpose. You are chosen for this work. (1 Peter 2:9)

Personally, from an early age, I felt a profound calling on my life. This experience helped me become aware of who I was supposed to be, not just who I was at the time, but who I was meant to become. I fell in love with Jesus at an early age. When I played outside with other children, I often took on the role of the preacher or the judge.

When I attended church, I always took things seriously. My grandmother had a huge family Bible with all sorts of pictures in it, which drew me and my curiosity to Jesus, angels, and everything about God and the Kingdom of God. However, I was not a perfect child; I did what everyone else around me was doing, but I always felt an extraordinary pull on my life. This pull has shaped my life in profound ways.

There were moments when I felt an inexplicable sense of purpose, even though I couldn't fully understand it at the time. One particular event that stands out is during a Gospel Quartet rehearsal at my grandmother's home. The Holy Spirit took control of me, and I danced throughout her whole house. My grandmother instructed everyone present not to touch me. She told everyone that what was happening was the Lord's doing. From that moment, I recognized a distinct change in the course of my life and became aware that I was meant to pursue a specific purpose.

As I grew older, I faced numerous challenges that tested my faith and resolve. There were times when I felt inadequate and unsure of my path. However, I came to realize that these moments of inadequacy were actually signs that I was being prepared for something greater. Some situations that I found myself in were shameful, but each challenge helped me grow stronger and more resilient.

One day, after experiencing so many trials, I gave up and surrendered to the Divine will of God. He met me right where I was, cleaned me up from sin sickness, and made me an instrument of His love for His people. There are vessels of honor and vessels of dishonor. I am glad to be counted as one of honor. The change that He made in my life reinforced my belief that I was on the right path. These experiences were like beacons of light, guiding me through the darkness.

Today, I can see how this early calling has shaped my life. It has given me a sense of purpose and direction that I might not have found otherwise. I have been able to effect change in the lives of others through sharing my testimony and the life that I now live in Christ.

In conclusion, this early calling has been a cornerstone of my journey. It has taught me the importance of faith, resilience, and trust in a higher power. I hope that by sharing my testimony, I can inspire others to recognize and embrace their own callings.

Especially to you: Engaging in Ministry

You are not an afterthought in the mind of God.
You are a special byproduct designed especially by His hands, to bring Him pleasure. It is with great regard that God has chosen to give you as a gift for His glory, for ministry work and not to build other men's visions simply. God will not allow the misuse of your gifts, talents, and fine qualities by others, and He never uses but utilizes your gifts and abilities and rewards you faithfully. You are someone of importance and someone special to Him. He needs you, but you need Him even more! He loves, appreciates, and esteems you to the highest. Just do not take His goodness and blessedness for granted. To God Be the Glory, forever, and ever and ever more.

Hallelujah!

Humbly yours in Christ,

Joyce Myrick Brown

Introduction

The purpose of this book is to offer guidance and information to those engaging in ministry, with a special emphasis on inclusivity for both men and women. In over thirty years of ministry and working in one capacity and then another, I have heard and seen so many things transpire concerning individuals who endeavor to engage in ministry. So many people have opinions that they feel are right, especially concerning those who feel compelled to answer the call. It is sad to say that there are so many varying opinions concerning this subject. The countless undeserved, ill-implemented, and unintended hurtful thoughts have contributed to unnecessary abuse in this area."

Challenges faced by people in the ministry include:

Gender and Position Opposition: Women often face opposition regarding their roles in ministry. There are individuals who remain unconvinced that women should fully engage in ministry, especially in higher positions such as Ordained Elder, Pastor, Bishop, or Apostle. This opposition can lead to feelings of isolation and unnecessary elimination from the ministry.

1. **Overcoming the Over-Rating View of Glamorous or Prestigious Positions**: Women in ministry may struggle with the perception that certain positions are glamorous or prestigious. This can lead to a desire for these positions based on their appeal rather than a genuine calling. It is important for women to stay focused on their true calling and not be swayed by external influences.

2. **Educating the Mind About Its Role in the Body**: Women need to understand their role in the body of Christ and overcome societal biases and issues that concern their position in ministry. This includes validation and affirmation through the word of God and effective discipleship.

3. **Acknowledging Your True Self**: Women in ministry must acknowledge

their true selves and affirm their identity in Christ. This involves accepting their undistorted identity, affirmation, and reinstatement as defined by God through His word.

4. **The Challenge of Being a Truthful and Genuine Minister of the Gospel**: Women in ministry must strive to be truthful and genuine in their service to God. This includes displaying Christlikeness in their conduct, avoiding meddling in others' affairs, and offering encouragement and wisdom.

5. **The Challenge of Educating Your Mind on Your Position in the Body**: Women need to understand their role in the body of Christ and overcome societal biases and issues that concern their position in ministry. This includes validation and affirmation through the word of God and effective discipleship.

By addressing these challenges, women in ministry can overcome obstacles and fulfill their calling with confidence and grace.

Here are some usual challenges that men face in ministry:

1. **Balancing Authority with Humility**: Men in ministry often struggle with balancing their authority and leadership roles with humility. It is important for them to lead with a servant's heart and avoid becoming overly authoritative.

2. **Connecting with Diverse Audiences**: Men in ministry may face challenges in connecting with diverse audiences, including different age groups, cultural backgrounds, and genders. Effective communication and empathy are key to overcoming this challenge.

3. **Navigating Societal Perceptions of Male Leadership**: Men in ministry may encounter societal perceptions and expectations regarding male leadership. They need to navigate these perceptions while staying true to their calling and maintaining integrity.

4. **Balancing Ministry and Family Responsibilities**: Men in ministry often face the challenge of balancing their ministry responsibilities with their family commitments. It is important for them to prioritize their family while fulfilling their ministry duties.

5. **Overcoming Feelings of Inadequacy**: Men may struggle with feelings of inadequacy and unworthiness when answering the call to ministry. Proper education, training, and mentorship can help them overcome these feelings and

fulfill their calling with confidence.

6. **Dealing with Opposition and Criticism**: Men in ministry may face opposition and criticism from others, including those who question their leadership abilities or disagree with their approach. It is important for them to stay focused on their mission and seek support from their community.

By addressing these challenges, men in ministry can overcome obstacles and fulfill their calling with confidence and grace.

Despite these differences, the shared thread is a call to serve God wholeheartedly and to bring His kingdom to the forefront.

With sincere prayers and heartfelt desire, I present to each of you this instrument, 'NUGGETS.' I present it in a manner that will enhance and motivate both male and female genders on each side of the spectrum, in a way that will guide toward a more comprehensible understanding of what it is to be specifically chosen by God for the unique and special work of the ministry, in all its facets."

I encourage you, the reader, to apply an open mind, to glean a higher, more in-depth understanding, to reach high and to go far beyond what these pages have to offer, and that you might be most effective in all you endeavor to do for the upbuilding of God's kingdom work in the earth and for His Glory!"

The introduction of "NUGGETS" emphasizes the purpose of the book, which is to offer guidance and information to those engaging in ministry, with a special emphasis on women. The author shares individual experiences from over forty years of ministry, highlighting the unique challenges faced by women in this field. The introduction also addresses the varying opinions and undeserved criticisms that women in ministry often encounter. The author presents the book as an instrument to enhance and motivate both men and women, guiding them towards a deeper understanding of their calling and the unique work of ministry. The introduction encourages readers to approach the book with an open mind, aiming to be most effective in their ministry work for the upbuilding of God's kingdom.

A Call to Action

NUGGETS: A Guide for Women Engaged in Ministry includes several calls to action. Here are some key examples:

- **Encouragement to Apply an Open Mind**: The introduction encourages readers to apply an open mind, to broaden a higher, more in-depth understanding, and to reach beyond what the pages offer to be most effective in their ministry work.

- **Challenge to Recognize and Respond to the Call**: The section on recognizing the call challenges individuals to make their calling and election sure, emphasizing the importance of proper education and training to become effective anointed leaders.

- **Advice to Consider Motives**: The book recommends that individuals examine their motives before engaging in ministry to ensure they are not acting on emotional impulses or external influences.

- **Encouragement to Stay Focused on the Assignment**: The book encourages readers to stay focused on their assignment, do their work in the anointing of the Holy Spirit, and do it with all that is within them.

The Challenge of the Call & Recognizing the Call

Here, we discuss the various challenges individuals face when answering the call to ministry. Here are some key points:

- **Universal Challenge**: Regardless of gender, ethnicity, or life positioning, everyone faces the challenge of answering the call to ministry. The enemy confronts individuals with challenges to prevent them from willingly giving themselves to the Master's use.

- **Sense of Unworthiness**: Many individuals struggle with feelings of unworthiness and inadequacy when considering the call to ministry. This can be due to a lack of correct teaching, misconceptions, and religious distortions.

- **Examples from Scripture**: The book provides examples from scripture, such as Moses, who questioned his worthiness and adequacy for the task of leading God's people. Other examples include Joshua, Elisha, Joseph, Abigail, and Jesus Christ, who all underwent proper training and preparation before engaging in ministry.

- **Importance of Education and Training**: Proper education and training are emphasized as crucial elements for becoming effective anointed leaders. This preparation helps individuals understand their purpose and equips them for the task.

The Calling: How It Manifests

The call to ministry often comes as a stirring within—an undeniable sense that God has a purpose and work set before you. This calling looks different for each person, shaped by individual gifts, circumstances, and seasons of life.

Scriptural Reflection:

"For we are co-workers in God's service; you are God's field, God's building."

1 Corinthians 3:9

The Challenges of Ministry

Every ministry journey is marked by challenges:

- Spiritual: Staying spiritually nourished while pouring into others.
- Personal: Facing self-doubt, rejection, or burnout.
- Practical: Managing time, resources, and relationships while fulfilling ministry responsibilities.
- Cultural: Navigating gender expectations or cultural barriers in the ministry field.

Understanding and addressing these challenges is essential to thriving in the ministry. They are not obstacles meant to defeat us but opportunities to deepen our reliance on God.

Section I: Part A

The Challenge of the Call

As stated by Peter,

"Wherefore the rather, brethren, give diligence to make your calling and election sure: for if ye do these things, ye shall never fall: For so an entrance shall be ministered unto you abundantly into the everlasting kingdom of our Lord and Savior Jesus Christ."
(2 Peter 1:10-11 KJV)

Regardless of who we are, our gender, ethnicity, or positioning in life, we individually face the challenge of answering the call to ministry. The enemy never intends for any one of us to give ourselves willingly to and for the Master's use. Therefore, he confronts us with challenges. In other words, when there is a definite calling on an individual's life, he or she tends to struggle with the mere thought of answering that call, of seeing themselves worthy of such a call, especially entering the ministry.

The challenge consists of various confrontations, including facing up. So many conflicting drawbacks concern people. A great portion of this is because of a lack of correct teaching, misconceptions, and religious distortions prior to and during the inception of the thought of working in the ministry. Drawbacks serve to point out our shortcomings, disadvantages, problems, downsides, negative aspects, and or weaknesses.

Moses was a fitting example of this. Moses asks himself the question, "Who am I?" to represent God and His chosen people. Who am I that I should go and confront the Pharaoh of Egypt?

I have heard others expound on this sense of unworthiness found in Moses. This was a good response. It examined his sense of worth or value in the likeness of Almighty God, as well as the leader of the nation of Egypt. In addition, it came to his mind that he would be inadequate for the task of becoming the great deliver because of his speech impediment.

There are even those of us who have pointed out the drawback of inadequacy. Initially, I felt inadequate in some areas.

Many people don't realize that sometimes inadequacy is a sign of being prepared for divine service. The enemy hates our security and thrives on deception, taking advantage of people. However, a secured and prepared vessel is very dangerous for the devil in the Kingdom of God, unlike a vessel that acts recklessly.

When we think of the threat we pose to the enemy, we can understand why answering the call would be an issue. Inadequacy can be one of the factors that hinder us from responding to a call. In fact, this could be an extensive list. On the other hand, this is the purpose of becoming equipped for the task. Proper education and training are designed to intercept and to sharpen our awareness of who we are and God's purpose for our lives. Education and training should be paramount for individuals seeking to pursue or feeling a vocation in the ministry. This is a crucial element of becoming an *effective anointed leader*.

We have seen grave outcomes of individuals who have entered the ministry without a divine calling or adequate training. So-called "mama-called" or "daddy-sent" persons are usually pushed into ministry by family tradition, emotional hype, or community expectation. They had little or no divine ordination or proper preparation for this service. Hence, these ministries suffer spiritual ineffectiveness, emotional burnout, doctrinal confusion, and abuse of authority. Ministry is not a career path to choose, but a divine mandate to confirm and develop as well.

Summary Box

- All of the above are feelings used by the enemy to delay or distract those with an authentic calling.
- Adequate and proper education and training should be in place for one to fulfill God's purpose with clarity and confidence.
- Do not enter the ministry out of family expectation (being "mama-called" or "daddy-sent"). Seek God for confirmation.
- If a ministry is not divinely called or prepared, the chances are high that it will do more harm than good.

Recognizing the Call

This text addresses the significance of recognizing and engaging with the call to ministry. Here are some key points:

- **Scriptural Foundation**: The scripture says, "For many are called, but few are chosen," (Matthew 22:14). It emphasizes the need to make one's calling and election sure, as stated in 2 Peter 1:10, "...make your calling and election sure: for if ye do these things, ye shall never fall."

- **Proper Instructions**: This book highlights that God never calls an individual into ministry without giving them proper instructions before sending them forth. Preparation is essential to avoid confusion and failure.

- **Exemplary Examples**: This book also provides examples of individuals from the Bible who received proper training and preparation before engaging in ministry. These include Moses and Joshua, Elijah and Elisha, Joseph, David, Paul, Jesus, Abigail, Deborah, and Anna the Prophet.

- **Protocol Steps**: The protocol steps of answering the call and entering the ministry consist of:

  1. Acknowledging the call
  2. Proving oneself as called
  3. Being placed in position/ministry by leadership.

- **Training and Preparation:** The book emphasizes the importance of training and preparation, like the approach taken by the biblical figures mentioned. This includes receiving guidance and mentorship from experienced leaders.

- **Examples of Training**: Nuggets provides specific examples of training periods for biblical figures:

  o Joshua received his training from Moses for forty years during the wilderness experience.

  o Elisha received his training from Elijah and came into the fruition of his

Prophetic Ministry twelve years after leaving his father's field.

- o Joseph experienced his dreams coming true after thirteen years following the actions of his brothers.

- o Jesus Christ, our Lord, and Savior did not exempt Himself from proper training. He acknowledged His call at twelve but waited for the appointed time, preparing for His earthly ministry.

The scripture says,

"For many are called, but few are chosen," (Matthew 22:14).

In all actuality, there are those who are "mama called" because Johnnie is a good old boy, "daddy sent" because I paid for his education, while others just got up and went. Our introductory scripture admonishes us to

"...make your calling and election sure: for if ye do these things, ye shall never fall: (2 Peter 1:10).

God always provides clear instructions before calling someone into ministry. People must be prepared; otherwise, we will make a terrible mess of ourselves. Responding in this way causes confusion and failure. It places the one in the lead position in a dangerous place that will end in serious misconception, with the end resulting in debauchery.

There are adequate exemplary examples on record for us, such as Moses and Joshua, Elijah and Elisha, Joseph, David, Paul and Jesus, Abigail, Deborah, Anna the Prophet, and others. Not one of these individuals engaged in the work of the ministry without adequate training or preparation for the office or position of his or her calling. Following the call or acknowledgment of our communication, we must then prepare accordingly for the subsequent call, like the approach taken by those I previously mentioned. The protocol steps of answering the call and entering the ministry consist of 1) acknowledging the call, 2) proving yourself as called, and 3) being placed in position/ministry by leadership.

Let us look more closely at the life of the above-mentioned by way of their tutelage and or the length of their training, such as:

Joshua

- Joshua received his training from Moses for forty years during the wilderness experience. He was trained, anointed, appointed, and assigned. This marks his calling and positioning in the ministry. He became Moses' successor.

Joshua received his training from Moses for forty years during the wilderness experience. This period of training was crucial for Joshua's development as a leader and his preparation for the responsibilities he would later undertake. Moses mentored Joshua, providing him with guidance, wisdom, and practical experience in leading the Israelites.

During this time, Joshua was trained, anointed, appointed, and assigned to various tasks. He observed Moses' leadership and learned how to navigate the challenges of leading a large group of people through difficult circumstances. This firsthand experience allowed Joshua to develop the skills and qualities necessary for effective leadership.

Joshua's training culminated in his appointment as Moses' successor. When Moses passed away, Joshua was ready to take on the mantle of leadership and lead the Israelites into the Promised Land. His training under Moses equipped him with the knowledge, confidence, and spiritual foundation needed to fulfill his calling.

Joshua's journey from being a mentee to becoming a leader is a powerful example of the importance of mentorship and preparation in ministry. It highlights the value of learning from experienced leaders and being equipped for the tasks ahead.

How it can be applied today:

Aspiring ministry leaders today can adopt a similar strategy by enrolling in church-based leadership programs, Bible colleges, or seminaries. In the same way that Joshua yielded to Moses' authority, believers today gain spiritual protection and guidance prior to taking on leadership duties.

Now the question is, has God assigned a mentor and guide to you in your calling? Do you actively submit to their training and leadership?

Elisha

- Elisha received his training from Elijah. He did not come into the fruition of his Prophetic Ministry until twelve years after leaving the field of his father to follow Elijah. He became Elijah's successor.

Elisha received his training from Elijah for twelve years after leaving his father's field to follow Elijah. This period of training was crucial for Elisha's development as a prophet and his preparation for the responsibilities he would later undertake. Elijah mentored Elisha, providing him with guidance, wisdom, and practical experience in prophetic ministry.

During this time, Elisha observed Elijah's leadership and learned how to navigate the challenges of being a prophet. This firsthand experience allowed Elisha to develop the skills and qualities necessary for effective prophetic ministry. Elisha's training culminated in his appointment as Elijah's successor. When Elijah was taken to heaven, Elisha was ready to take on the mantle of leadership and continue the prophetic ministry. His training under Elijah equipped him with the knowledge, confidence, and spiritual foundation needed to fulfill his calling.

Elisha's journey from being a mentee to becoming a leader is a powerful example of the importance of mentorship and preparation in ministry. It highlights the value of learning from experienced leaders and being equipped for the tasks ahead.

How it can be applied today:

Just like Elisha, believers today gain great benefits from practical discipleship under seasoned ministers. Pastoral internships and prophetic schools are designed to sharpen spiritual gifts, and lay ministry settings are among places where this can take place.

Now the question is, are you ready for God to use your life in a public way? Are you prepared to serve and learn even during times when it is hidden?

Joseph

- Joseph, the eleventh son of Jacob, experienced his dreams coming true after thirteen years following the actions of his brothers. Sold into Egypt and worked as a hired servant of Potiphar. Lied on by Potiphar's wife, suffered imprisonment and finally gained recognition from the Pharaoh to interpret his dream. He became the second greatest man of Egypt, rising to the position of Governor.

Joseph's journey began with his dreams, which foretold his future leadership and the reverence his family would show him. However, his brothers' jealousy led to his being sold into slavery in Egypt. This marked the beginning of a series of challenging experiences that would prepare him for leadership.

In Egypt, Joseph worked as a hired servant for Potiphar. Despite his difficult circumstances, Joseph remained faithful and diligent, earning Potiphar's trust and rising to a position of responsibility. However, Potiphar's wife falsely accused Joseph, leading to his imprisonment. Even in prison, Joseph's integrity and leadership qualities shone through, as he gained the trust of the prison warden and was put in charge of other prisoners.

Joseph's ability to interpret dreams eventually brought him to the attention of Pharaoh. When Pharaoh had troubling dreams, Joseph was called upon to interpret them, demonstrating his wisdom and insight. Impressed by Joseph's abilities, Pharaoh appointed him as the second greatest man in Egypt, rising to the position of Governor. This role allowed Joseph to implement strategies that saved Egypt and surrounding nations from famine.

Throughout his journey, Joseph's experiences of betrayal, slavery, false accusations, and imprisonment were instrumental in developing his leadership skills. These challenges taught him resilience, humility, and the importance of relying on God. Joseph's story is a powerful example of how adversity can shape and prepare individuals for significant leadership roles.

How it can be applied today:

Like Joseph, some modern leaders are molded in the shadows, by miscommunication, false charges, or adversity. Formal education and seminary are important, but so are the wilderness seasons, which develop character and teach perseverance.

Are you resisting the process, or are you letting your present struggles prepare you for the future?

Abigail

- Abigail, a seasoned woman of God, had applied herself to know and to understand the mind and ways of God. Even King David revered her as a woman of wisdom. After the death of her husband Nabal, she became one of the wives of David and an advisor to the King.

Abigail was a seasoned woman of God who played a significant role in King David's life. Here are some key points:

Abigail was known for her wisdom and understanding of God's ways. She was married to Nabal, a wealthy but foolish man. When Nabal refused to help David and his men, Abigail took it upon herself to intervene. She prepared a generous gift and went to meet David, offering wise counsel and urging him not to take vengeance on Nabal. Her actions not only prevented bloodshed but also earned David's respect.

After Nabal died, Abigail married David and became a trusted advisor, valued for her wisdom and insight. Abigail's story is a powerful example of how a woman's wisdom and faithfulness can have a profound impact on those around her.

How it can be applied today:

Abigail serves as a symbol for many devout women in leadership positions, counseling, and lay ministry today who employ spiritual discernment to guide their choices. Bible studies and Christian women's leadership programs can foster this kind of influence.

How are you intellectually and spiritually getting ready to be a wise voice in your church or community?

Jesus

- Jesus Christ, our Lord, and Savior did not exempt Himself from proper training. He first made known His acknowledge of the call when He was twelve, but submitting to the guidance of His parents, He waited for the appointed time, all the while preparing for His earthly ministry. He studied as a Rabbi of the Jewish faith, and at the age of thirty, he began his ministry. He further stressed His view of the importance of training-by-training His disciples.

Jesus Christ, our Lord and Savior, underwent significant training and preparation for His ministry. Here are some key points:

Jesus first made known His acknowledgment of the call when He was twelve years old. During this time, He was found in the temple, discussing with the teachers and demonstrating His understanding of the scriptures. However, He submitted to the guidance of His parents and waited for the appointed time to begin His ministry. This period of waiting was crucial for His preparation.

Throughout His early years, Jesus studied as a Rabbi of the Jewish faith. He immersed Himself in the scriptures and gained a deep understanding of God's word. At the age of thirty, He began His ministry, fully prepared and equipped for the tasks ahead. His training emphasized the importance of proper preparation and understanding of one's calling.

Jesus further stressed His view of the importance of training by training His disciples. He spent three years training his disciples, equipping them with the skills needed for future ministry.

Jesus' journey from acknowledging His call to beginning His ministry is a powerful example of the importance of mentorship and preparation in ministry. It highlights the value of learning from experienced leaders and being equipped for the tasks ahead.

How it can be applied today:

Even Jesus gave in to a period of time for growth, learning, and preparation. Today, ministry schools, pastor-led mentoring, and spiritual retreats all work toward developing ministers before sending them out into the world.

Before beginning your ministry assignment, are you prepared to accept the preparation season and wait for God's allotted time?

Other challenges to confront.

Remember, women engaged in ministry (WEIM) as well as men engaged in ministry (MEIM) have their challenges. In which I caution you to take courage, be strong, and to endure hardness as a good soldier of the gospel. You will face several challenges, including:

- *Overcoming the over-rating view of a glamorous or prestigious position*
- *Gender and position oppositions*
- *Educating the mind about its role in the body*
- *Acknowledging your true self*
- *The affirmation of who you are in Christ.*
- *Reinstatement as defined by God through His word.*
- *The challenge of being a truthful and genuine minister of the gospel.*

Summary Box

- Calling must be recognized, confirmed, and followed with training.
- The steps: acknowledge the call, prove the call, and be placed by leadership.
- Skipping divine calling or preparation leads to misplaced leadership and possible destruction.
- Endurance, mentorship, and correct positioning are critical for long-term impact in ministry.

The Challenge of Overcoming the Desire of Glamorous or Prestigious Positioning

Being involved in ministry as a male or female is appealing. We should not allow these appeals to become our motivation for becoming a part of the ministry. Various areas of ministry are glamorous or prestigious from the outset. Nowadays, we see those in Christian leadership are often surrounded by an entourage of people, and it sends off such a charismatic effect that can be luring for people.

For instance, you will see the Bishop, Apostle, Evangelist, Prophet, or Pastor arriving for an appointment with a crowd gathered around him or her. My advice for this is to those engaging in ministry, not to become entangled in the mix. While there is nothing necessarily wrong with such an encasing, it should not become the drawing appeal to become the call of God. Keeping in the forefront of the mind, the entourage is there for a purpose, which is to serve their leaders, not as a God, but as those called to the ministry of helps/to assist.

As for women, we often see the fashionable dress attire; the pretty, big, and fancy hats, the gorgeous shoes and handbags worn by the elite women in our local churches, throughout our localities, states and on television among those who hold the position of first lady, missionary, teacher, evangelist, elder, or pastor. In the midst of all this glamour, we become overwhelmingly impressed.

We as people are often impressed with what we see on the outside and therefore hastily desire to share in the glimmer of the perception we think we see, without being fully aware of what it took the individuals to get to where they are. Sad to say, we more often than not fail to realize that there is a story behind the story. We are outsiders looking in and desiring to become. We seldom understand the internal struggles, ridicule, self-doubt, and challenges to their sense of worth that individuals may have faced on their journey to their current positions.

While on the onset, the various offices may appear to be all "peaches and cream," I assure you that it is not by any stretch of the imagination. Therefore, I encourage everyone endeavoring to venture into these chartered waters to be certain that you are not answering to an emotional impulsion, or an influence passed on to you by someone else, or by the prestige of the office itself. This is not an unreliable adventure; it is a life-long endeavor, and those who engage in it must be committed to the call. Become fully aware of yourself and your motives. So, search yourself and your motives before becoming engaged in ministry.

Actionable steps:

To assess your heart posture, have a spiritual mentor conduct a "motives check-in" every three months. Create a daily devotional routine to ground your purpose on Christ rather than outward appearances. Reflect on your inner goals and emotional tendencies by keeping a notebook.

The challenge of gender and position opposition

In varying cases, there is the sting of persecution. There are those (male and female) who remain unconvinced that a woman should fully engage in Ministry. There are those of you who may have no problem being accepted on the level of the Missionary, Teacher, and Evangelist, but not on the level of Ordained Elder, Pastor, and not Bishop or Apostle, and do not dare to venture into the area of Deacon. Therefore, prepare to meet with the opposition in these areas.

In addition, remember this is not a call to engage in physical combat and confrontations. We do not have the time or the need to prove ourselves by engaging in word battles, and so forth. This will only lead to isolation and unnecessary elimination from the body, which in effect defeats our ultimate purpose and goal.

Be watchful of the ploy of others who come to pull you out of character. As Christian men and women engaging in ministry, our primary goal is to assist those who are struggling with sin, entanglements, and the realization of their authentic self in Christ. So, make every effort; do not lose focus in this area by confrontations among the genders. My advice for the best way to avoid such situations is to stay prayed-up, studied-up in the word, and faith-up. Only God, through His beloved Son Jesus and by the *dunamis unction* and *power* of the Holy Spirit, will establish and prove you to the world, for His glory and grace.

Challenges Faced by Men vs. Women in Ministry

Category	Men	Women
Perception of Authority	Often expected and supported	Frequently questioned or challenged
Leadership Acceptance	Easier access to pastoral roles	Often limited to supportive or secondary roles
Public Image Pressure	Pressure to remain strong, decisive	Pressure to balance appearance, family, and ministry
Emotional Expression	Discouraged or seen as weak	Expected but often used to undermine credibility
Mentorship Access	More access to male mentors	Limited access, especially in conservative spaces
Theological Legitimacy	Rarely questioned	Often asked to "prove" their calling through scripture
Opposition within Church Culture	Occasionally due to theology or politics	Regularly based on gender, appearance, and traditional roles
Support Networks	Broader availability	Must be intentionally created or joined
Spiritual Expectations	Leading prayer, preaching, oversight	Nurturing roles, intercession, supporting vision

Actionable steps:

Take part in training on emotional intelligence and conflict resolution. Participate in or start a ministry support group that includes male allies to have open conversations about common objections. Every day, repeat biblical affirmations to strengthen your sense of self and purpose.

The challenge of educating your mind on your position in the body.

I understand that the eminent role of male and female is a prevalent issue in our society. In fact, a subject deemed adequately and effectively addressed, which lands Christendom on the threshold of fully taking in hand certain biases and issues that concern women and their position in the ministry work of Christ and His church. Along these lines, I feel our initial approach should include first validation and or affirmation. This validation and affirmation come through the word of God and through an effective discipleship, which teaches the word of God from an unbiased perspective, as understood in the following areas:

a. *Man (humankind) created in the image of God.*

When we read the Word of God from the Genesis perspective of the creation of humankind, we clearly see God had a distinct purpose and plan. Genesis, 1:27 states,

> *"So God created man in his own image, in the image of God created he him; male and female created he them."* **(Gen 1:27 KJV)**

In Genesis 5: 1-2 the scripture tells us that,

> *"In the day that God created man, in the likeness of God made he him; male and female created he them; and blessed them, and called their name Adam, in the day when they were created."*

As we revisit the first chapter of Genesis, see the empowering position, and duties of humankind. In equal capacities as stated in the twenty-eight verse

"And God blessed them, and God said unto them, Be fruitful, and multiply, and replenish the earth, and subdue it: and have dominion over the fish of the sea, and over the fowl of the air, and over every living thing that moveth upon the earth." **(Gen 1:28 KJV)**

b. *Sin's results in a distorted view and alteration of order*

However, the original order of God, because of the fall of man *(humankind)* in the garden, seriously altered creation's plan. In effect, over the course of time, the value of women and her role in the grand scheme of things has veered, while the value and role of men have remained the same. Various distorted views of women have existed within the religious sector and are now in need of being rectified. Again, this rectification comes from God alone as revealed through His Word. We must take into consideration all the influences that have gone into humankind's system of thought.

c. *The view of the world versus the truth of God.*

After the garden experience, the fall, and humankind having to leave the garden, man went through different transitions. Therefore, we must consider the man Abraham, and his background in paganism before his encounter with God; the years his descendants spent in Egypt and their experiences there as well as the influences of that nation upon the minds of a people who only had a relationship with Almighty God through Abraham, and who had not yet developed a fellowship.

In other words, they until this point in time could only relate to the knowledge passed down to them by their ancestors. They yet had to come to know Him God for themselves. This relationship established through the man Moses, and the experience of exodus became the implementation of this course of action.

d. *A defining moment in Biblical History concerning the female gender.*

Abraham's descendants had to exit Egypt before coming to a place of knowing God for their selves. One of the things that they came to know about God was His view of women, His daughters. A realization arrived through a need and the act of provision, i.e., there was a situation to occur while dividing the land among the twelve sons (descendants) of Jacob, the Israelites.

The book of Numbers contains a story about the daughters of Zelophehad who spoke to Moses regarding their inheritance. Until this time in history, the request made by Zelophehad's daughters went to their sons. However, it is indisputable as to how God views His daughters as seen in the following account:

> *¹ Then came the daughters of Zelophehad, the son of Hepher, the son of Gilead, the son of Machir, the son of Manasseh, of the families of Manasseh the son of Joseph: and these are the names of his daughters; Mahlah, Noah, and Hoglah, and Milcah, and Tirzah. ² And they stood before Moses, and before Eleazar the priest, and before the princes and all the congregation, by the door of the tabernacle of the congregation, saying, ³ Our father died in the wilderness, and he was not in the company of them that gathered themselves together against the Lord in the company of Korah; but died in his own sin, and had no sons. ⁴ Why should the name of our father be done away from among his family, because he hath no son? Give unto us therefore a possession among the brethren of our father. ⁵ And Moses brought their cause before the Lord. ⁶ And the Lord spake unto Moses, saying, ⁷ The daughters of Zelophehad speak right: thou shalt surely give them possession of an inheritance among their father's brethren; and thou shalt cause the inheritance of their father to pass unto them. ⁸ And thou shalt speak unto the children of Israel, saying, if a man dies, and have no son, then ye shall cause his inheritance to pass unto his daughter"* **(Numbers 27:1-8 KJV).**

The story of the daughters of Zelophehad is a significant example of how God views His daughters and their rights. Here are some key points:

The daughters of Zelophehad were Mahlah, Noah, Hoglah, Milcah, and Tirzah. Their father, Zelophehad, had died in the wilderness and had no sons. According to the customs of the time, inheritance typically passed through male descendants. However, the daughters of Zelophehad approached Moses, Eleazar the priest, the princes, and the congregation to request their father's inheritance. They argued that their father's name should not be done away with simply because he had no sons. Moses brought their case before the Lord, and the Lord responded, affirming that the daughters of Zelophehad were right. God instructed Moses to grant them a possession of inheritance among their father's brethren. Furthermore, God established a new law stating that if a man dies and has no son, his inheritance should pass to his daughter.

This story is a powerful example of God's fairness and justice, demonstrating that He values His daughters and ensures their rights are upheld. It highlights the importance of advocating for one's rights and the willingness of God to listen and respond to the needs of His people.

This one story so adequately describes the sentiments of God's heart for (his daughters) women who are in the faith and in right standing with Him.

God gave the antidote of redemption to restore humankind to His preferred state.

Yes, it is true, humankind failed in the garden, and woman played a pivotal role in the fall, but God has not eternally and stripped her for this act, nor has God eternally and stripped man. Instead, He implemented an antidote for their situation to reinstate them to their position to fulfill His plan and purpose in and through them.

Yet, to fulfill this purpose, we must first be affirmed (*both male and female*), and that affirmation comes through the word of God, which is through the Sacrificial Lamb, Jesus Christ, and His atoning death on the cross and resurrection from the dead for our sins. For the scripture says,

> *"That if thou shalt confess with thy mouth the Lord Jesus, and shalt believe in thine heart that God hath raised him from the dead, thou shalt be saved"* **(Romans 10:9 (KJV).**

Actionable steps:

Enroll in certificate programs or theological studies that emphasize women in ministry. Create a weekly Bible study group that examines gender justice in the Bible, or join one already in existence. For inspiration and a theological foundation, read about the women who have led the church throughout its history.

The challenge of accepting your undistorted identity, affirmation, and reinstatement.

Our reinstatement with God through Christ brings us back into right standing and in proper position. God made both the male and female in His own image with the purpose of cohabitation, to jointly share in dominion over all things in the earth and to reproduce their own kind. The role of woman in terms of more adequately defining the word *helpmeet* is to share in complementarity to man in all things of God. When we fail to look at the role, position, and place of the two from this perspective, we come away with a distorted view.

There is something else of relevance that we must be mindful of concerning women engaging in ministry. Because of the fall, things are out of order. Although our identity is established and affirmed as daughters in equal relationship with our male counterparts, and that we are not afterthoughts in the mind of God, still, there are those who would have us believe that there is still a divine order of things.

- There is a fact that not every woman has a husband. As a result, there are cases wherein women are heads of families because of absentee fathers in our homes.
- However, in lines of proper positioning where there is a husband and wife/family, Christian wives and children should give proper respect to the headship in the household.
- Then there are occasions where women are in leadership on their jobs, or in their careers, which includes the church. These women can operate in these capacities as adequately as any man does, because God made and equipped them to do so. A great biblical example of this is Deborah, found in Judges 4. In addition, there is Pricilla and Aquila, who, on occasions where these two are mentioned, her name is mentioned first, which was due to the pivotal role of leadership she displayed in collaborating with the Apostle Paul and the establishment of the first-century church.

Actionable steps:

Take part in identity-based devotionals that highlight your place in Christ, such as Ephesians 1. For more profound inner healing and confidence strengthening, get in touch with a spiritual counselor. To validate callings, participate in workshops for women in leadership.

The challenge of truthfulness and genuineness

This is a position of highest regard. Remember, as WEIM, this is a work of service and of giving glory to God by the good works He has called you to do. The conduct of WEIM is not that of self-exhortation or a position of overachievers of the more competitive, ambitious strivers. Do not take this opportunity for granted.

You will need to know and to trust your core values and your place in the Lord. Remember, our goal is to always display Christ's likeness in the way that we conduct ourselves privately or publicly. We are workers together with Him, Christ, one in the Spirit, and singleness of mind and heart.

We should avoid meddling in others' affairs or gossiping. Instead, we offer encouragement, enlightenment, and wisdom. As members of WEIM, we are role models for others. Our purpose is to serve as ministers and conduits of grace on behalf of God Almighty Himself. Remember, there are so many who will look to you and depend on you to be there for them. You must therefore

"Serve wholeheartedly, as if you were serving the Lord, not men" (**Ephesians 6:7**).

Actionable steps:

Take part in identity-based devotionals that highlight your place in Christ, such as Ephesians 1. For more profound inner healing and confidence strengthening, get in touch with a spiritual counselor. To validate callings, participate in workshops for women in leadership.

The commission to mission

The Lord told the servant to go into the streets and urge people to come in, so the house can be filled (Luke 14:23 KJV). You have been commissioned on a mission.

The heart of God toward the lost, the disregarded, and those beyond the conventional folds of the church is reflected in this divine instruction, which the Lord gave. Reaching out beyond one's comfort zone and into the roads, byways, and areas where people live in spiritual need is exemplified by the picture of the servant being sent into the streets. The instruction to "encourage them to come in" conveys sincerity, zeal, and a sense of urgency in completing this task.

You have been commissioned on a mission. This is a divine mandate from the Lord Himself, not just a recommendation. In order to fill God's house, it places a strong emphasis on acting, going out, seeking, inviting, and pushing souls to join the fold. It is an appeal to all believers, not only members of the clergy or the leadership, but to everyone who is a member of Christ's body.

Being involved in the growth of God's kingdom is both a divine obligation and an open invitation. We are all given a part to play in the harvest, whether that part is by preaching, teaching, serving, encouraging, or just lending a helping hand and sharing our stories.

This is an internal as well as external mission. It pushes us to pursue love, compassion, and obedience above and beyond religious obligation and habit. The Lord's house will be full and His will be carried out through our hands, our words, and our lives when we obey this commission.

Actionable steps:

Set weekly objectives for outreach, such as prayer walks, personal invitations, and deeds of kindness. Keep an "invitation log" in which you record and pray for each individual you extend an invitation to. Collaborate with other ministries to launch evangelistic campaigns throughout the city.

Taking The Step

Now, in taking this step into the call of work to ministry, there are things you need to know or be aware of. The main ingredient for success will be found in your attitude. Attitude means everything.

A **(WEIM)** must be a lover of people. Although it may not always be easy, it is possible through prayer and consecration.

A **(WEIM)** must not be a busybody, but a keeper of your own home, minding well your own affairs.

A **(WEIM)'s** mission and vision must coincide with that of her pastor's. Therefore, she must know the vision and goal of her pastor, who heads the local church.

A **(WEIM)** must know that she has been called into a special work that may also include leadership of others, as well as other women. Eyes will be upon her; therefore, she must set an example in the way she presents herself. She, therefore, must lead a quiet, godly life, and she must respect those in authority.

A **(WEIM)** unless otherwise positioned as the Bishop, Apostle, or Pastor; as a leader in the under-shepherd ministry, she must remind herself to faithfully serve under the guidance and care of her local church leader, pastor, president, and others. Or the designated department overseer in the local church.

Remember, in any position of the church ministry, you are assigned or appointed by the leader. In other words, you can confess to experiencing a call from God on your life, but unless you are walking in alignment and allegiance with your pastor, that position does not ever have to be realized in that assembly. God is not the author of confusion, and He does not work out of order for anyone. He placed pastors in position to oversee His churches, and those who serve in any capacity of the under-shepherd's ministry are under the pastor's authority. Your life of service in good standing is essential to fulfilling the will and purpose of God in your life.

Defining Ministry roles and positions within the local church assembly of today

What Is Ministry? Ministry is more than a role; it is a calling. It is a divine invitation to serve others, share God's word, and reflect His love through actions and leadership. While ministry takes on many forms, at its core, it is an act of obedience to God's calling and a response to His purpose for our lives.

Ministry is not confined to a pulpit or a church building; it is lived out in homes, workplaces, communities, and beyond. It is a balance between spiritual devotion, personal sacrifice, and practical service, and it often challenges individuals to grow beyond their comfort zones.

Scriptural Foundation:

"But you are a chosen people, a royal priesthood, a holy nation, God's special possession, that you may declare the praises of Him who called you out of darkness into His wonderful light." **(1 Peter 2:9)**

"Each of you should use whatever gift you have received to serve others, as faithful stewards of God's grace in its various forms." **(1 Peter 4:10)**

The Calling: How It Manifests

The call to ministry often comes as a stirring within—an undeniable sense that God has a purpose and work set before you. This calling looks different for each person, shaped by individual gifts, circumstances, and seasons of life.

Scriptural Reflection:

"For we are co-workers in God's service; you are God's field, God's building."

1 Corinthians 3:9

Roles and positions, male and female roles and positions Ephesians 4:11~13

The Office of the Apostle - The Office of the Prophet - The Office of the Evangelist - The Office of the Pastors and the Office of the Teacher

The Five-Fold Ministry:

The Office of the Apostle

The office of the Apostle is one of the five-fold ministry gifts. Apostles are called to establish and oversee churches, provide spiritual guidance, and ensure the proper functioning of the ministry. They are often seen as pioneers, laying the foundation for new ministries and guiding them towards growth and stability.

Apostles are responsible for teaching and training other leaders, helping them to develop their spiritual gifts and fulfill their calling. They also play a crucial role in maintaining doctrinal purity and addressing any issues that may arise within the church.

The role of the Apostle is not limited to a specific gender. Both men and women can be called to this office and serve effectively in this capacity.

The Office of the Prophet

The office of the Prophet is one of the five-fold ministry gifts. Prophets are called to deliver God's messages to His people, often providing guidance, correction, and encouragement. They play a crucial role in discerning God's will and communicating it to the church and its leaders.

Prophets are responsible for speaking forth God's word with boldness and clarity, often addressing issues that others may overlook or avoid. They help to maintain the spiritual health of the church by ensuring that God's voice is heard and His will is followed.

The role of the Prophet is not limited to a specific gender. Both men and women can be called to this office and serve effectively in this capacity.

The Office of the Evangelist

The office of the Evangelist is one of the five-fold ministry gifts. Evangelists are called to spread the gospel and share the message of salvation with others. They play a crucial role in reaching out to those who may not have heard the gospel and bringing them into the fold of the church.

Evangelists are responsible for preaching and teaching the word of God with passion and conviction. They often travel to various places, conducting revivals and evangelistic meetings to reach as many people as possible. Their ministry is focused on winning souls and making disciples.

The role of the Evangelist is not limited to a specific gender. Both men and women can be called to this office and serve effectively in this capacity.

The Office of the Pastors

The office of the Pastor is one of the five-fold ministry gifts. Pastors are called to shepherd and care for the congregation, providing spiritual guidance, support, and leadership. They play a crucial role in nurturing the spiritual growth of the church members and ensuring the proper functioning of the ministry.

Pastors are responsible for preaching and teaching the word of God, offering counsel and support to individuals, and overseeing the various activities and programs within the church. They help to create a sense of community and belonging among the congregation, fostering an environment where members can grow in their faith and develop their spiritual gifts.

The role of the Pastor is not limited to a specific gender. Both men and women can be called to this office and serve effectively in this capacity.

The Office of the Teacher

The office of the Teacher is one of the five-fold ministry gifts. Teachers are called to instruct and educate the congregation, providing deep insights into the scriptures and helping believers to grow in their understanding of God's word. They play a crucial role in nurturing the spiritual growth of the church members and ensuring that the teachings of the Bible are accurately conveyed.

Teachers are responsible for preparing and delivering lessons, facilitating discussions, and encouraging critical thinking among the congregation. They help to create a sense of community and belonging among the church members, fostering an environment where individuals can grow in their faith and develop their spiritual gifts.

The role of the Teacher is not limited to a specific gender. Both men and women can be called to this office and serve effectively in this capacity.

Section I - Part B
Description of Levels of Offices

Female-Defined Ministry Workers In the Church of Today

The Aspiring Missionary

The Aspiring Missionary is the first level of Women Engaged in Ministry (WEIM) within the local church. This role is designed for individuals who feel a strong call of God upon their lives to work in ministry. The title "Aspiring Missionary" derives from the idea of one aspiring to become and who is willing to go through the process required to become who the individual aspires to be.

Usually, various church settings involve the Aspiring Missionary as a young woman of legal age, who has presented herself in good Christian standards, and who walks in alignment and allegiance with leadership. She strongly feels a special call of God on her life. Her life must be that of a Godly example. She must be concerned about her church. She must be a woman of prayer and a strong believer in the study and application of the Word of God. She must be a woman capable of teaching the word and have a love for soul winning, as well as one who feels the inner call to the service of God.

A woman entering this phase of the ministry must be observed for a specific period, which may require a length of at least two years under the watchful eye of her pastor. During this time, part of her requirements would include attending workshops and other training classes recommended by her leader before moving into the next position, which is that of the Licensed Missionary.

Other criteria for an Aspiring Missionary include:

- Confessing to salvation, sanctification, and being filled with the Holy Ghost.
- Proving herself faithful, practicing self-control, and possessing a good moral standard of conduct.

- Studying to show herself approved unto God, rightly dividing the word of truth.
- Having a true concern for God's people, encouraging those who are part of her local church as well as anyone she may meet.
- Participating in church activities, praying, and being able to teach.
- Being actively involved in the soul-winning ministry of her church.
- Being knowledgeable of the doctrine of her church, the church's mission, and its protocol.
- Attending and participating in Sunday/Church School, Bible Study, Pastoral Services, and regularly scheduled services.
- Knowing what appropriate dress attire is for specific occasions.
- Serving within the confines of her local church, but with the permission of her pastor, she may serve outside the church with accompaniment.

Upon completion of observation by her pastor and proper training, the Aspiring Missionary will then be examined by her pastor, the supervisor of the WEIM, and/or the Board of Examiners. If she passes the examination, she will then become a Licensed Missionary.

The Licensed Missionary

The Licensed Missionary is one who has gone through all the phases of an Aspiring Missionary and has served well in this capacity. Her life should be that of a woman of God who has applied herself to the study of the Word of God as her rule of faith and practice, seeking knowledge from God and training through Institute Classes, Bible School, or other recognizable forms of Christian education. This will better equip her to serve God and His people.

Her purpose is to serve her local church and to help build the work of God in the Women's Department, which will enhance the general work. The Licensed Missionary, as recommended, however, not necessarily the norm, after two years of in-service training, if led by God, her activities could lead to the Evangelist Ministry.

The Licensed Missionary/Evangelist is one who has successfully gone through the phases of an Aspiring Missionary and a Licensed Missionary, and whose ministry extends outside the local church assembly into other church settings upon invitation as a speaker. It is important to note here that not all Evangelist Missionaries have outside engagements. However, to fill any outside speaking engagements, she must have the endorsement of her pastor.

The expectations of the Licensed Missionary/Evangelist are to help build the work of her local church on all levels. Also, she must be available to travel and conduct revivals wherever or whenever called upon.

An Evangelist Missionary will have two prerequisites:

- **A Mission**: A mission defines her area of ministry work more clearly. The area of ministry work is the area in which the one called will hear the cry of ministry the most.
- **A Vision**: A vision gives focus that will guide the one called in on how to accomplish the mission.

These two prerequisites are necessary and will support the achievement of the mission and increase effectiveness.

The Licensed Missionary Evangelist

The Licensed Missionary Evangelist is one who has successfully gone through the phases of an Aspiring Missionary and a Licensed Missionary, and whose ministry extends outside the local church assembly into other church settings upon invitation as a speaker. It is important to note that not all Evangelist Missionaries have outside engagements. However, to fill any outside speaking engagements, she must have the endorsement of her pastor.

The expectations of the Licensed Missionary Evangelist are to help build the work of her local church on all levels. Also, she must be available to travel and conduct revivals wherever or whenever called upon.

An Evangelist Missionary will have two prerequisites:

- **A Mission:** A mission defines more clearly her area of ministry work. The area of ministry work is the area in which the one called will hear the cry of ministry the most.
- **A Vision:** A vision gives focus that will guide the one called in how to accomplish the mission.

These two prerequisites are necessary and will support the achievement of the mission and increase effectiveness.

National Evangelist

It is important to note that the ministry of the Evangelist is one of the five-fold ministry gifts. The Evangelist Ministry may be included with the Missionary's Ministry or regarded as being like, yet this office is not to be conducted entirely as that of the missionary.

A National Evangelist is one who is qualified and endorsed by her pastor.

She is one who has been called to go out and travel into various areas outside of the state in which she lives. Yet, her home base is her local church, where she is supportive.

WEIM on this level are resolute and set apart to God with extraordinary gifts and the anointing of the Holy Ghost for the service of winning souls. She is one who has had the opportunity to address congregations in more than three States, and if opportunity presents, she has addressed a congregation outside the United States of America on at least one occasion.

We realize and respect the fact that in various church structures, the candidate for evangelist does not receive a license, but rather, is ordained into this position.

We encourage all Evangelists to seriously consider attending a Bible College or to take courses in certain areas of evangelism so you can be Bible literate and have a good world-view knowledge and perspective when standing before God's people. One may not know the educational level of the audience you may address, so we want to prepare ourselves with all people in mind.

A full-time Evangelist must secure a benefits package that includes health insurance and social security, given the travel and speaking engagements involved.

Section II

Descriptions, Course Requirements and Duties of the Licensed Minister, Ordained Elder, Deacon and the Deaconess

Ministry Positions (non-biased gender roles) Acknowledged in the Church of Today

The Aspiring Minister or Minister in Training (MIT)

The Aspiring Minister or Minister in Training (MIT) is a crucial role within the local church assembly. This position is designed for individuals who feel a strong call of God upon their lives to work in ministry. The title "Aspiring Minister" derives from the idea of one aspiring to become and who is willing to go through the process required to become who the individual aspires to be.

Usually, various church settings involve the Aspiring Minister as a young person of legal age, who has presented themselves in good Christian standards, and who walks in alignment and allegiance with leadership. They strongly feel a special call of God on their life. Their life must be that of a Godly example. They must be concerned about their church. They must be a person of prayer, and a strong believer in the study and application of the Word of God. They must be capable of teaching the word and have a love for soul winning, as well as one who feels the inner call to the service of God.

An individual entering this phase of the ministry must be observed for a specific period, which may require a length of at least two years under the watchful eye of their pastor. During this time, part of their requirements would include attending workshops and other training classes recommended by their leader before moving into the next position, which is that of the Licensed Minister.

Other criteria for an Aspiring Minister include:

- Confessing to salvation, sanctification, and being filled with the Holy Ghost.
- Proving themselves faithful, practicing self-control, and possessing a good moral standard of conduct.
- Studying to show themselves approved unto God, rightly dividing the word of truth.
- Having a true concern for God's people, encouraging those who are part of their local church as well as anyone they may meet.
- Participating in church activities, praying, and being able to teach.
- Being actively involved in the soul-winning ministry of their church.
- Being knowledgeable of the doctrine of their church, the church's mission, and its protocol.
- Attending and participating on Sunday/Church School, Bible Study, Pastoral Services, and regularly scheduled services.
- Knowing what appropriate dress attire is for specific occasions.
- Serving within the confines of their local church, but with the permission of their pastor, they may serve outside the church with accompaniment.

Upon completion of observation by their pastor and proper training, the Aspiring Minister will then be examined by their pastor, the supervisor of the ministry, and/or the Board of Examiners. If they pass the examination, they will then become a Licensed Minister.

The Licensed Minister

The Licensed Minister has a crucial role within the local church assembly. Here are some key points about the responsibilities and duties of a Licensed Minister:

Licensed Ministers are trained by pastors as they are part of the ministerial staff of a church. They participate in and conduct religious services. A recognized Minister is usually acknowledged as an ambassador, one who is sent as a representative of church affairs. In most situations, the Minister is often placed in charge of and is required to take care of the needs of the people they are assigned to. Licensed Ministers, in most cases, can receive an appointment by their leader as an appointed pastor of a congregation even before becoming ordained to the position of an Elder. However, this is not the rule for all churches. In any event, the Minister may, at a designated time, be ordained to Eldership. A Minister is one called to serve and is apt to teach and/or preach. A Minister can perform a wedding ceremony; however, only with an accompanying official clergy member in attendance. The official is an Ordained Elder or Reverend who can sign legal contracts such as the Marriage License. A Minister can also perform a eulogy at a funeral if requested by a family.

The Ordained Elder

The office of the Ordained Elder is one of the highest positions in the church, second only to that of the pastor. In various church settings, this role is often part of a board comprised of qualified individuals who have met both spiritual and moral requirements and who have acknowledged the call of God upon their lives. A candidate for Elder cannot be a novice but must be one who has come up through the ranks, been examined, and proven worthy by the pastor because of their stewardship toward the gospel and the affairs of the church.

This position is a lifetime commitment on the part of the candidate, as well as a lifetime appointment from God. Ordination to Elder is a prestigious reward for those who reach this level, recognizing all the preparation and endurance required to attain this position.

The Elder's work includes:

- **The Word of God**: Elders are responsible for teaching and preaching the Word of God, ensuring that the congregation receives sound biblical instruction.
- **The Sacraments and the Orders of the Church**: Elders oversee the administration of sacraments such as Communion and Baptism, as well as other church ordinances.
- **The Oversight and Care of the Flock of God**: Elders provide spiritual guidance and care for the congregation, ensuring their well-being and growth in

faith.

The charge to the Elder is outlined in 1 Peter 5:1-4, which emphasizes the importance of willingly taking on the responsibility of overseeing the flock of God, not for personal gain but with a ready mind and as examples to the congregation. When the Chief Shepherd appears, the Elders will receive a crown of glory that does not fade away.

The bishop

The office of the bishop is a significant and esteemed position within the church. Bishops are responsible for overseeing multiple congregations, providing spiritual guidance, and ensuring the proper functioning of the ministry. They play a crucial role in maintaining doctrinal purity, addressing any issues that may arise within the church, and providing leadership to other church leaders.

Bishops are often seen as shepherds, guiding their flock with wisdom and compassion. They are responsible for ordaining ministers, overseeing church activities, and ensuring that the church's mission is conducted effectively. The role of the bishop is not limited to a specific gender. Both men and women can be called to this office and serve effectively in this capacity.

The responsibilities of a Bishop include:

- Providing spiritual oversight and guidance to multiple congregations.
- Ensuring the proper administration of sacraments and church ordinances.
- Ordaining ministers and providing mentorship to church leaders.
- Addressing doctrinal issues and maintaining the integrity of the church's teachings.
- Overseeing church activities and ensuring that the church's mission is conducted effectively.

The role of the bishop is a lifetime commitment and requires a deep understanding of God's word, strong leadership skills, and a heart for serving God's people. It is a position of great honor and responsibility, and those who are called to this office are expected to lead with humility, integrity, and dedication.

The Missionary Pledge

- The Holy Bible is the word of God, which, as stated in II Timothy 2:15, which are inspired by Him for His purpose and our good. I accept it to be the infallible, authoritative revealed will of God.

- I hold its truth dear and close to my heart.

- I believe in the doctrine of the Bible and trust it is accurate teaching of this church as it is interpreted by our founder, (Pastor, Leader) and perpetuated by the ordained Elders which are the guardians of the doctrine and upheld by the ministers of this church to be the doctrinal and principal guideline for which we are to be governed.

- I, therefore, pledge to teach it faithfully.

- I will teach no other doctrine for as long as I hold office as a Woman Engaged in the Ministry Work (WEIM) of this church.

- I also pledge my loyalty to the leadership of this church.

- I will always hold my pastor and those in authority in esteem, highest honor, and regard.

- I further pledge my obedience and service to the best of my ability in all that I do according to God's Holy WORD.

The Position of the Deacon & the Deaconess

The Position of Deacon

The role of Deacons is referenced in several scriptures in the Bible. Here are some key references:

- **Acts 6:1-6**: This passage describes the selection of the first deacons in the early church. The apostles appointed seven men to serve and assist in the daily distribution of food to the widows, allowing the apostles to focus on prayer and ministry of the word.

- **1 Timothy 3:8-13**: This passage outlines the qualifications for deacons. It emphasizes the importance of being dignified, not double-tongued, not addicted to much wine, not greedy for dishonest gain, and holding the mystery of the faith with a clear conscience. It also mentions that deacons must be evaluated and found blameless before serving.

- **Philippians 1:1:** In this verse, Paul addresses the saints in Philippi, along with the overseers and deacons, highlighting the role of deacons in the church.

These scriptures provide a foundation for understanding the role and qualifications of deacons in the church. The role outlined in this book encompasses a range of responsibilities, duties, and functions. The following are the key highlights:

- **Service and Support:** Deacons are called to serve and support the church community. They assist in various church activities and ensure that the needs of the congregation are met, Such as outings in the park, Community Programs, and services, etc.
- **Care for the Congregation:** Deacons are responsible for caring for the sick, shut-ins, and those who are less fortunate. They prepare care packages and deliver them to the homes of those in need.

- **Assistance at Church Services:** Deacons assist at church services, including Communion and Baptismal Services. They ensure that everything is prepared and that the services run smoothly.

- **Support for the Pastor:** Deacons often assist the pastor during church services, providing necessary support and ensuring that the pastor's needs are met.

- **Home Visits:** Deacons make home visits, especially to those who are unable to attend church services. They provide spiritual support and encouragement to these individuals.

- **Teamwork with Deaconess:** A Husband-and-Wife team as Deacon and Deaconess are considered precious gems, especially when they receive proper training for the position and work in unison together.

- **Biblical Example:** Paul acknowledged the Deaconess Phoebe of the church at Cenchrea, commending her as a servant of the church and a helper of many, including himself (Romans 16:1).

The Position of Deaconess

Praise God for the Deaconess. Paul acknowledged the deaconesses in the early church who were a part of the official church staff. Most churches, after careful and prayerful examination, the pastor, to this position, appoints these individuals. The role of Deaconess is referenced in several scriptures in the Bible. Here are some key references:

- **Romans 16:1-2:** Paul acknowledges the Deaconess Phoebe of the church at Cenchrea, commending her as a servant of the church and a helper of many, including himself. He writes, "I recommend to you our sister Phoebe, a deacon of the church in Cenchreae. I request that you welcome her to the Lord in a manner befitting His followers and provide any assistance she may require, as she has been a benefactor to many individuals, including myself.

- **1 Timothy 3:11:** This verse outlines the qualifications for women who serve in the church, which can be applied to Deaconesses. It states, "In the same way, the women are to be worthy of respect, not malicious talkers but temperate and trustworthy in everything."

These scriptures provide a foundation for understanding the role and qualifications of Deaconesses in the church.

The Deaconess is entrusted with a variety of responsibilities and ceremonial duties. The following key functions are among those assigned to her role:

- **Preparation and Assistance at Communion Services:** The Deaconess prepares and assists at the church's Communion Services.

- **Assistance at Baptismal Services:** The Deaconess assists at Baptismal Services and advises on appropriate attire for baptism. She ensures that everyone understands the proper clothing used for the candidates, especially the female candidates.

- **Care for Baptismal Robes:** The Deaconess is responsible for having the baptismal robes cleaned after the service and ready for future candidates.

- **Care for the Sick and Shut-Ins:** The Deaconess Ministry cares for the sick, shut-ins, and those who are less fortunate by preparing care packages and delivering them to the homes of those in need.

- **Appointment by the Pastor:** The leader or pastor appoints the Deaconess to this position.

- **Altar Worker and Intercessor:** The Deaconess is an Altar worker, intercessor, and prayer warrior. She stands in the gap for those who cannot stand for themselves.

- **Attendance to the Pastor:** The Deaconess usually attends to the pastor during the Sunday morning Worship Service, ensuring that the pastor is well attended by providing necessities.

- **Accompanying the Deacon:** The Deaconess accompanies the Deacon when he makes home visits, especially when visiting the homes of other females[9].

- **Husband-and-Wife Team:** A Husband-and-Wife team as Deacon and Deaconess are considered precious gems, especially when they receive proper training for the position and work in unison together[10].

- **Biblical Example:** Paul acknowledged the Deaconess Phoebe of the church at Cenchrea, commending her as a servant of the church and a helper of many, including himself (Romans 16:1).

Paul admonished the Deaconess Phoebe of the church at Cenchrea.

"I commend to you sister Phoebe, a servant (which is referred to as deaconess in this passage) of the church at Cenchrea, that you may receive her in the Lord as befits the saints and help her in whatever she may require from you, for she has been a helper of many and of myself as well." **(Romans 16:1)**

All Deacons, male or female (inclusiveness), should go through training in the areas appointed to work prior to performing in that area of ministry. In various cases, a one-day workshop will be appropriate.

Remember, in all areas of (WEIM), we should know our protocol dress code. Uniformity is important. It shows that we as WEIM are with one accord. Wearing proper attire shows that we care. We care about ourselves; we care about our leaders and the church, and of course, we all care about how our Heavenly Father sees us. Let whatever we do or say display unity so that the ministry is blameless in anything.

Each of us should be privy to the same information and training in our home church so we can give the same presentation to the body of Christ when we are before the public. Training in all areas of Ministry is essential. We cannot afford the risk of someone thinking they know something to be correct, only to be in error.

Recommended Course Requirements for Those Engaging in Ministry

All who are engaging in Effective Ministry, before receiving a license or ordination, must have completed courses in Old and New Testament Surveys of the Bible, Hermeneutics, and most definitely Public Speaking, and or Homiletics.

The Five-Fold Ministry

- The Office of the Apostle
- The Office of the Prophet
- The Office of the Evangelist

National Evangelist - includes the following:

- Homiletics
- Revivalist
- The Office of the Pastors
- The Office of the Teacher

Aspiring Missionary

- Church Etiquette
- Church Protocol
- Women in the Bible-Old Testament
- Women in the Bible-New Testament
- Knowing Your Bible (an introduction to the Word of God)
- Altar Training

(The above courses must be completed within two years).

Licensed Missionaries

- Old Testament Survey
- New Testament Survey
- The Writings of Paul
- Hermeneutics
- Public Speaking

(The above courses are for completion within two years).

Missionary Evangelist ~ includes the following:

- World Missions
- Evangelism

Dress Code

Every church has a proper dress code for those engaged in the ministry. There is usually a different uniform for each office level. Ministerial colors are usually black and white throughout. Dress styles should vary to distinguish diverse groups.

On Official Days

On official days, all officers are required to wear ministerial dress attire. A pin worn on the lapel of a suit jacket can also be proven helpful in making distinction between each ministerial level.

Appearance:

- Look attractive, business like, not sexy, or flirtatious.
- Preferably wear suites with modest hemlines, (no stiletto heels).
    - You want men to respect-you not struggle to keep their flesh under.
    - If you are unsure of what to wear or of your choice of outfits, always get a second opinion from another (WEIM).

Ministers and Elders should wear uniforms during official procedures. The chief adjutant usually informs clergy members of the proper attire.

Tips for public appearance and comfort for WEIM

- Never chew gum when on an assignment.
- Always keep mints for your breath.
- Always keep feminine products near for your personal hygiene.
- Wear comfortable shoes; in fact, always wear an extra pair.
- Wear a robe or take an extra outfit on speaking engagements, especially Evangelists, Ministers, and Elders.
- Always be sensitive to the sensitivity of those you are ministering to.
- Be particularly sensitive to others' sensitivity when wearing various fragrances, deodorants perfumes, and other things that can be annoying.
- Always carry a traveling companion with you. Remember, Jesus sent them out in twos.

Section III

Required Study Part A

Ministry Positions (non-biases gender roles) Acknowledged in the Church of Today

The Minister Elect

The required course of study for the Minister Elect is on the same level as that of the Aspiring Missionary and Licensed Missionary. His or her endeavors are to aspire to become a licensed Minister, fully engaging in the ministerial areas of the local church's operations. Those engaged in this level of the Ministry are preparing to fulfill the office of the Licensed Ministry and the position to which his or her Pastor/leader will commit them into his or her care.

The Minister Elect

- Old and New Testament Survey of the Bible
- Hermeneutics
- The Writings of Paul
- Public Speaking
- Pulpit Etiquette
- The Church Structure/The Minister's Role

The First Year Licensed Minister

Required course of study should include not limited to,

- Homiletics
- The Minister's Role/Communion
- The Minister's Role/Funeral Procedures
- The Minister's Role/Procedures of a Marriage Ceremony
- The Minister's Role/Baptismal

Courses such as these are available through Seminars or Workshops as approved by their Pastors.

Required course of study for the deacon, male, or female (inclusive):

All Deacons, male or female (inclusiveness), should go through training in the areas appointed to work prior to performing in that area of ministry. In various cases, a one-day workshop will be appropriate.

Remember, in all areas of (WEIM), we should know our protocol dress code. Uniformity is important. It shows that we as WEIM are with one accord. Wearing proper attire shows that we care. We care about ourselves; we care about our leaders and the church, and of course, we all care about how our Heavenly Father sees us. Let whatever we do or say display unity so that the ministry is blameless in anything.

Each of us should be privy to the same information and training in our home church so we can give the same presentation to the body of Christ when we are before the public. Training in all areas of Ministry is essential. We cannot afford the risk of someone thinking they know something to be correct, only to be in error.

The Purpose of License and Ordination

All born-again believers have a call to minister to the lost, to pray for the sick, to feed the hungry, as well as other things. We really do not need to be ordained or have a license to do so. However, the proper credentials make three distinct statements of the acknowledgement, which are:

- The statement of the acknowledgement of the call of God on a worker's life.
- The statement that your spiritual leader acknowledges this call and therefore has licensed or ordained you to the position in which you will now serve.
- The statement to the world that you are a qualified worker. Your credentials will open doors for you, allowing you access to various places you could not have

gone to otherwise.

Here's Your Interview

Here is a section that places emphasis on asking or interviewing individuals about themselves and their perspectives on ministry:

Interviewing Individuals Engaged in Ministry

To gain a deeper understanding of the experiences, perspectives, and motivations of individuals engaged in ministry, it is essential to conduct interviews that explore their personal journeys, challenges, and insights. Here are some suggested questions to guide these interviews:

1. Personal Background and Calling:
   - Can you share a bit about your background and what led you to pursue a calling in ministry?
   - How did you first recognize your calling, and what steps did you take to respond to it?

2. Experiences and Challenges:
   - What were some of the most significant experiences in your ministry journey?
   - Can you describe any challenges you have faced and how you overcame them?

3. Perspectives on Ministry:
   - How do you define ministry, and what does it mean to you personally?
   - What do you believe are the most important qualities for someone engaging in ministry?

4. Impact and Goals:
   - How has your ministry work impacted your life and the lives of others?
   - What are your goals for your ministry, and how do you plan to achieve them?

5. Inclusivity and Diversity:
   - How do you ensure that your ministry is inclusive and welcoming to people of

all genders, backgrounds, and cultures?

o   What role does diversity play in your ministry, and how do you address it?

6. Advice for Aspiring Ministers:

o   What advice would you give to someone who is considering answering the call to the ministry?

o   How can aspiring ministers prepare themselves for the challenges and responsibilities of ministry?

7. Spiritual Growth and Development:

o   How do you continue to grow and develop spiritually in your ministry work?

o   What practices or habits have been most helpful in nurturing your spiritual life?

8. Collaboration and Community:

o   How do you collaborate with other ministry workers and leaders to achieve common goals?

o   What role does the community play in your ministry, and how do you foster it?

By asking these questions, you can gain valuable insights into the personal journeys and perspectives of individuals engaged in ministry. This will help create a more comprehensive and inclusive understanding of the subject.

Worksheets
Part B

Making Preparation for Ministry

These are specific questions designed for this course on your worksheet:

Making Preparation for Ministry. Take your time, pray, and reflect on your study, as you pursue engaging in ministry and how you will fulfill the requirements as presented.

1. What inspired you to pursue a calling in ministry?

_____

_____

_____

_____

2. How do you define your personal mission and vision for your ministry work?

_____

_____

_____

_____

3. What steps have you taken to prepare yourself spiritually, mentally, and emotionally for ministry?

_____

_____

_____

_____

4. How do you plan to balance your ministry responsibilities with your personal life and family commitments?

_____

_____

_____

_____

5. What challenges do you anticipate facing in your ministry, and how do you plan to address them?

_____

_____

_____

_____

6. How do you intend to engage and connect with diverse audiences within your ministry?

_____

_____

_____

_____

7. What role does mentorship play in your preparation for ministry, and who are your mentors?

_____

_____

_____

_____

8. How do you plan to continue your education and training in ministry to stay effective and relevant?

_____

_____

_____

_____

9. What are your goals for the first year of your ministry, and how do you plan to achieve them?

_____

_____

_____

_____

10. How do you intend to measure the success and impact of your ministry work?

_____

_____

_____

_____

Defining Your Spiritual Gifts Worksheet

1. What spiritual gifts do you believe you have been given?

    o   Reflect on your experiences and identify the gifts you feel you possess.

    _____

    _____

    _____

    _____

2. How have you used your spiritual gifts in your ministry work?

    o   Provide examples of how you have applied your gifts in various ministry activities.

    _____

    _____

    _____

    _____

3. What impact have your spiritual gifts had on your ministry and the people you serve?

    o   Describe the positive outcomes and changes you have observed because of using your gifts.

    _____

    _____

    _____

    _____

4. How do you plan to further develop and enhance your spiritual gifts?

o   Outline the steps you will take to grow and strengthen your gifts.

_____

_____

_____

_____

5. What challenges have you faced in using your spiritual gifts, and how have you overcome them?

o   Share any obstacles you have encountered and the strategies you used to address them.

_____

_____

_____

_____

6. How do you discern when and where to use your spiritual gifts?

o   Explain your process for determining the appropriate times and places to apply for your gifts.

_____

_____

_____

_____

7. What role do prayer and seeking God's guidance play in using your spiritual gifts?

o   Discuss the importance of prayer and divine direction in your ministry work.

_____

_____

_____

_____

8. How do you collaborate with others who have different spiritual gifts?

   o Describe how you collaborate with individuals who possess different gifts to achieve common ministry goals.

   _____

   _____

   _____

   _____

9. What scriptures or biblical principles guide your understanding and use of spiritual gifts?

   o Identify key verses or teachings that inform your approach to using your gifts.

   _____

   _____

   _____

   _____

10. How do you measure the effectiveness of your spiritual gifts in your ministry?

    o Explain the methods you use to evaluate the impact and success of your gifts.

    _____

    _____

    _____

    _____

The Statement of Faith Worksheet

(This Page Is Design for You to Write Your Church's Statement of Faith)

_____

_____

_____

_____

_____

_____

_____

_____

_____

_____

_____

_____

_____

_____

_____

_____

_____

_____

_____

_____

The Doctrine

Why We Believe? What We Believe?

"That we henceforth be no more children, tossed to and fro, and carried about by every wind of doctrine, by the sleight of men, and cunning craftiness, whereby they lie in wait to deceive, but speaking the truth in love, may grow up in Him in all things, which is the head, even Christ."
(Ephesians 4:14-15 KJV)

A. The word "doctrine" simply means to teach or to instruct.
B. A "biblical doctrine" is simply all that the Bible teaches or says about a particular subject.

Following is a list of Doctrinal truths observed in our churches.

- The Bible (The Word of God)
- The Father God (Theology)
- The Son Jesus (Christology)
- The Holy Ghost (Pneumatology) (The Spirit, the wind, the breath)
- The Doctrine of the Baptism of the Holy Ghost
- The Doctrine of the Church (Ecclesiology)
- The Doctrine of Man (Anthropology)
- The Doctrine of Sin (Hamartiology)
- The Doctrine of Salvation (Soteriology)
- The Doctrine of Angels
- The Doctrine of Satan (Satanism)
- The Doctrine of Demon (Demonology)
- The Second Coming of Christ
- Divine Healing
- Miracles
- Grace
- The Kingdom
- Last Things

Ordinances of the Church

What does your church teach concerning the following?

Please include scriptures for your reference.

Holy Communion

_____

_____

_____

_____

_____

_____

_____

_____

Feet Washing

Not all churches recognize feet washing as one of the ordinances, it is not necessarily inched in stone practice. However, it is beautiful when practiced. It brings about a sense of intimacy, unity, and humbleness.

_____

_____

_____

_____

_____

_____

Water Baptism

_____

_____

_____

_____

_____

_____

The Spiritual Life

The Spiritual Life is a life that develops in the Holy Spirit through prayer and praise and the study of God's Word.

A. Develop a life of Prayer and Praise.

For helpful scriptural tips in prayer and praise, read the following scriptures:

Prayer	Praise
Luke 18:1	Psalm 33:1
I Corinthians 14:15	Psalm 34:1
Ephesians 6:18	Psalm 66:2
I Thessalonians 5:17	Isaiah 61:3

B. Know your Bible through study and application.

10 Points to a Successful Study in the Word

- Read God's Word.

- Get involved with Sunday/Church School.

- Read daily devotions.

- Look up scriptures that pertain to your present situation.

- Practice doing a Word search.

- Confess God's Word.

- Repeat the Word to yourself repeatedly when you have the opportunity.

- Share the Word with others.

- Do God's Word. Find ways that you can put God's Word in your daily life. At this point, you will find the true power of God's Word in action.

The Power in Knowing God's Word

A life applied to the study of God's Word is a life that is rich and filled with the blessings of God. God's Word is "Spirit and Life" (John 6:63).

"My people are destroyed for lack of knowledge" **(Hosea 4:6a)**

"The Lord gave the word: great was the company of those that published it" **(Psalm 68:11).**

"...Even to the time of the end; many shall run to and fro and knowledge shall increase." **(Daniel 12:4b)**

"Study to shew thyself approved unto God, a workman that needeth no to be ashamed, rightly dividing the word of truth." **(II Timothy 2:15)**

C. Know the Plan of Salvation

Isaiah 53:6
John 3:16
Romans 10:8-10, 13
Colossians 1:14
II Corinthians 5:17
Galatians 6:15 (RSV)
Read the booklet – "Five Spiritual Laws" by Bill Bright.

D. Fruit of the Spirit - Growth and Production

A godly man is compared to a tree planted by the rivers of life.

"His delight is in the law of the Lord, and in God's law he meditates day and night. And he will be like a tree that is firmly planted by streams of water, which yields its fruit in its season, and its leaf does not wither; and whatsoever he does, he prospers" **(Psalm 1:2-3)**

Jesus also compared our relationship with Him to that of the vine. Please read the following scriptures concerning our spiritual growth and production: John 15:4, 5

It is essential that we grow and produce, but the only way we can form and produce is through the Fruit of the Spirit, and against such there is no law. Galatians 5:22, 23

Studying the Fruit of the Spirit through scripture references. Allow the Spirit to work out the former fruits of the flesh (Galatians 5:19-21) and develop in the Fruit of the Spirit unto a better work for Christ.

The fruit of the Spirit develops character, personality, and attitude. Remember, it is our attitude that determines our aptitude in life.

Spiritual Gifts

The Gifts of the Spirit

Gifts of the Spirit are in the following books of the Bible:

- Romans 12:6-8

- I Corinthians 12:8-10

- Ephesians 4:11

I also read 1Peter 4:10 and 11, which also refers to the Gifts of the Spirit. These Gifts are in three categories:

- The Ministering Gifts

- The Gifts of Manifestation

- The Five-Fold Ministry Gifts

The Bible teaches that the Holy Spirit gives every redeemed person at least one gift. "Now there are varieties of gifts. But every member receives the manifestation of the Spirit for the common good (I Corinthians 12:4, 7).

DO YOU KNOW YOUR GIFT?

Writing helps you to affirm and express your beliefs.

(In the area below, please write out your Spiritual Gift)

_____

_____

_____

_____

_____

_____

_____

_____

_____

_____

_____

_____

_____

_____

_____

_____

_____

_____

_____

_____

_____

_____

Express In Writing Your Specific Calling

Express In Writing Your Affirmation of Calling

_____

_____

_____

_____

_____

_____

_____

_____

_____

_____

_____

_____

_____

_____

_____

_____

_____

_____

_____

_____

_____

_____

_____

_____

_____

Explanation of Calling

Do You Know the Names and Positions of the Leaders in the Local and National Church?

S. No	Name	Title

Protocol Is!

"Honor to whom honor is due." (Romans 13:7)

So, we ask the question, what does protocol mean? Well protocol means to esteem others, respect leadership, and the rules and guidelines set before you that are demonstrated through loyalty, dignity, integrity, status, gracefulness, and appearance.

The first rule in protocol is to:

- Respect leadership.

- Remember, to be a good leader, you must first become a good follower.

- Every (WEIM) is under the authority of her leaders unless she is the pastor or Bishop. Regardless, we are all accountable to someone else.

- We must submit ourselves to those who have the rule over us. Remember, because we have received a calling from God, it does not mean we are without rules.

- We must respect our leaders in our thoughts, in our words, and in our actions, whether in their presence or in their absence. God has an all-seeing eye, and His ears are attentive to whatever we say. He knows our hearts. He knows how we feel and how we think.

- We must always be mindful of the devices of Satan. If we are not careful of what we think and feel, satan will have us speak against our leaders rather than speak for them.

- We should pray that our thoughts are full of good things to say concerning our leaders.

- We should uphold our leaders and be ever mindful to esteem them highly. They keep us lifted before God in their prayers, so let us not make it grievous for them to lead us. Be careful of our body language in response to our leaders.

- We are **NOT** asking that you make the leader into God, for God is God alone, and we esteem Him high and above everything, no question about it. We ask that you honor and respect your leaders as desired by our Heavenly Father.

Proper protocol may require us to relinquish our seats or to stand when our leaders enter the room. It also teaches us to love one another because love constrains us to be like Jesus. Jesus did not overlook authority in His day. Each of us should want to be like Jesus. How was He? "Nevertheless, not my will but thine be done" (Luke 22:42b). Remember, "Ye are the light of the world. A city that is set on a hill cannot be hid" (Mathew 5:14). "Let your light shine before men, that they may see your good works and glorify your father which is in heaven" (Matthew 5:16).

Stewardship

A good steward is committed to Christ and displays his or her faithfulness in their service to Christ, the church, and others continually. Therefore, my beloved brethren, be ye steadfast, unmovable, always abounding in the work of the Lord, forasmuch as ye know that your labor is not in vain in the Lord, I Corinthians 4:2.

- A good steward is one who demonstrates their faithfulness and loyalty to both God, who has entrusted him, and to his leader to whom God has entrusted him.
- A steward is one to whom the power of management is entrusted.
- A steward is an individual who is delegated by an owner to govern or manage his owner's property and or household.

Webster's Dictionary describes a steward to be "a person entrusted with management of states or affairs not his own; an administrator." A good steward displays a life of principle and of faithfulness in their service to Christ and His church.

Examples of Biblical Stewards:

A Good and Faithful Steward

Abraham had a good and faithful steward whom he entrusted his affairs to. His name was Eliezer. Gen. 15:2; 4:1-9

An Unwise Steward: The prophet Elisha, on the other hand, had an unwise and unfaithful steward. 2 Kings 4:12; 5:20-27. Also read Acts 5:1-11 ~ Ananias and Sapphira.

The Steward in relationship with God:

- Knows God is the owner of all things.
- Knows that as the owner of all things, God is the giver of our source and

resources.

- Knows that he must give an account to God for all things entrusted to him.

- Knows God pays all debts owed. Regardless of your labor, He will reward us whether our deeds are good or bad; God will pay the debt owed.

As a steward, we are to give.

Our life to God, our time to God, our talents to God, our abilities to God, our possessions to God, our finances to God, our faithfulness to God, and our praise to God.

- All the glory for everything belongs to God.

God has invested a great gift within us. He has found us suitable for Him to entrust His

Word. Let us not falter in our walk or in our conduct as good stewards of the gospel. Therefore, let us hold fast to the standards of His teachings and the calling He has placed upon our lives.

History of Women in Ministry Then and Now

The following are examples of biblical women who obeyed and pleased God. Read the stories of the following women in the Bible.

Shiphrah and Puah (Exodus 1:15-21)

- Abigail (I Samuel 25)
- Deborah (Judges 4)
- Ester (Esther 4:11-16)
- Rahab (Joshua 2:3)
- Mary, the mother of Jesus

Also, there were other women of the early church. Read Acts 8:1-4

WEIM, since biblical times, includes such women as:

- Minnie Abrams (1859-1912).
- Mother Angelica (1923).
- Maria Atkinson (! 879-1963).
- Aimee Semple McPherson (1844-1924).

Research the works.

- Women who are currently engaged in ministry:
- Apostle Marian Jones
- Bishop Barbara Amos
- Pastor Pula White

- Prophet Juanita Bynum

- Teacher Joyce Myers

- Teacher Marilyn Hickey

There are others to include in your record of trailblazer women in ministry.

Most importantly, do not forget the women who labor among you. Do not forget the countless others (WEIM) who sit in your midst, or those you may meet on a regular basis. Always be mindful that there is no one greater than another. We are one, and together our purpose is to get the job done. The same God calls us to do a work unto His glory, and that not of ourselves. I encourage you to stay focused on the assignment that you have been appointed to do. Do your assignment in the anointing of the Holy Spirit and do it with all that is within you to do. Now I present you unto Him who can keep you from falling, and to present you faultless before His throne, our all-wise and eternal Lord and Saviour Jesus Christ.

God bless your every endeavor to do His will.

Joyce Myrick Wooden

Nuggets Of Gold

For the Excellency of the Ministry, remember, "a job worth doing is a job worth doing well," and in the times in which we are living, there is no reason we cannot do the best job possible for the service of man and to the glory of God. We have literature in abundance; we have computer technology, and so many more resources available. There is no excuse for failing in any area of the ministry that appointed us.

It is Time to Deliver

Those engaged in ministry, who are public speakers/preachers, should have a message to always deliver, no matter where she is at or for whatever the occasion. She should always be ready. Therefore, always be prepared. The process of being prepared:

1. **Preparation**-be always prepared!

   - Get quiet mentally.
   - Go fast.
   - Lay before the Lord in prayer.
   - Seek the Father for what it is He wants to say to His people.

2. **Search and Communicate–I Thessalonians 5:17**

   - Once you feel you are released and assured of the message you are to speak, search the scriptures, for it is foundational scriptures.
   - If you have problems finding the scriptures you need, always communicate.
   - Share your needs with your prayer partner. Between the two of you, you will find the appropriate scriptures.
   - Also, if you need help in formatting an outline for your message, ask and you shall receive the help needed.
   - An outline and proper formation will prove helpful when it is time to deliver.

3. Mediate on Psalm 1:2.

- To meditate means to let something roll repeatedly in your mind.
- Take time out to think about and to rethink what you will say to the Father for His children.
- Always take and keep your notebook with you.
- Always keep your notepad with you and take notes.
- Listen to what the Holy Spirit is conveying to your spirit.

Suggested Class Study Guide:

- The Redemptive Names of God
- The Words of Praise
- How to Structure and Deliver a Message
- Tithe and Offering
- Reports and Dues
- The Vision and Goal of the Church
- What Is the Difference Between Revelation, Inspiration, and Illumination?
- Is The Holy Spirit a Person or a Force?
- What Is Salvation?
- What Is the Central Message of Christ?

These topics suggest areas for in-house classes, seminars, or workshops to better equip your church's Women's Ministry.

As In Our Opening
Let us close with prayer.

Gracious God,

Thank You for the truths unveiled, for the quiet moments of conviction, and for the inspiration stirred within. As the *Nuggets* close, may it open new doors of intimacy with You. Let the wisdom gathered here ripple outward—into families, into communities, into the world. Seal these words in the heart of every reader. Let them walk away empowered, edified, and eager to live out what they have received. We trust that every soul drawn to these pages was led by You, and now, we send them forth covered by Your grace and guided by Your hand. Amen.